Bone
of
His
Bone

Bone
of
His
Bone

by

F. J. Huegel

Bone of His Bone
Copyright 1997 by Gene Edwards
Published by The SeedSowers
          P.O.Box 285, Sargent, GA 30275

Extensively revised and modernized by The SeedSowers
Cover illustration by Bill Johnson

Library of Congress Cataloging-in-Publication Data

Huegel, F.J.
          Bone of his bone / F.J.Huegel
          ISBN 0-940-232-596
          1. Spiritual Life.   1. Title
          Catalog Card Number:

Printed in the United States of America

Times New Roman 12pt

DEDICATION

To the memory of the precious child, now in glory,
who in the participation of the sufferings
incident to my missionary labors,
came so early to know the deep meaning of the cross.

Her Father

FOREWORD

One thing for the Christian worker is inevitable.

If you are to go forward in the face of the seemingly insuperable obstacles which await you, if you are to labor for that which is closest to the heart of God, then you must appropriate in an ever-deeper and fuller way the power of Christ.

You must be bound to that unconquerable Christ who, all down through the centuries, has achieved the impossible through His disciples.

You must move beyond a mere intellectual knowledge of Christ, and so entwine your spiritual nature into the eternal Christ that you absorb His divine life.

The task you are attempting requires superhuman force, that is, something human life does not effect. The merely human life, however noble and strong and cultivated, is insufficient and inadequate—as inadequate as a handful of glowing coals would be for the warming of an arctic blizzard. You must transcend the purely natural, and immerse yourself in the supernatural. You must experience the power of the indwelling Christ. You must lose your own life and discover the fuller measure in divine life, which is yours to experience.

Only "rivers of living water" flowing from your innermost being—the promise which the Savior has made to his own—can make possible the renewal of your life and the growth of

His greater life.

It may be that you are not inclined to forge your way into these lonely uplands of the faith. You may even have an aversion to the mystical elements of the Christian faith. Still the force of circumstances, like a mighty tide, may sweep you from the moorings of an intellectual grasp of Christian realties, casting you out into the depths of a vital experience of Christ and His grace. Christ must become more real to you than any other reality. He must become more real than the physical universe which surrounds you.

Learn to draw upon Christ and to sink your being into Him. You will emerge finding yourself in the deeper will of the living God. Then will you be charged with that power which fell upon the disciples of old.

Otherwise, you are, from the very nature of the circumstances in which you are involved, doomed to defeat. The force which you would overcome will rake destruction on your purpose.

This book is a simple outline of the experience to which I was led and my position which grew out of the experience. I wish to share with you my blessed experiences of the indwelling Christ. Here are immeasurable treasures which have become mine through a deeper union with Christ. I wish to make available my experiences of oneness with Christ, the very Christ without whom you can do nothing.

I cannot send forth these messages without acknowledging the great debt of gratitude which I owe the late Mrs. Penn-Lewis, who wrote on the deeper aspects of the Cross and on identification with Christ in death and in resurrection.

It is my prayer that you may be given grace to realize in your own experience this deeper oneness with Christ—that your joy may be that joy which is "unspeakable and full of glory," your peace that "peace which passeth all understanding," and your life that "abundant life" which is eternal and which flows from the throne of God.

I place these messages upon the altar of my Lord that He might use them for the building up of the holy ones and for the glory of His name.

F.J.Huegel

1

The Christian Life a Participation, Not an Imitation

As you study the New Testament you cannot but be shocked at the glaring difference between the modern Christian life and the ideal set forth by Jesus Christ.

When you compare the picture of the Christian life as set forth by the apostles with what we see today, you stagger. There is as much difference as exists between the emaciated body of a dying friend and a past photo showing him in days of health and vigor.

It is not my object to pick to pieces the modern Christian. My only purpose in calling attention to our failure is to point the way to the victorious life in Christ for those who are conscious of their spiritual poverty and who "hunger and thirst after righteousness."

If you search for the water of life, and are perhaps sick with yearning for it, I hope to unfold to you the secret of the abundant life—the life of which Jesus spoke when He said that rivers of living water would flow from your innermost being. If you are weary of hollow mockeries, sick of the shams, and have become the victim of self-loathing, a feeling that as a Christian you should be free from a sense of failure, it is to you that I long to bring the message of the Cross. This book is addressed to you who long to have your life and service, ministry and preaching, charged with the Spirit of the living God.

We are told that we cannot be Christ's disciples if we do not renounce ourselves utterly and absolutely in all things, and at all times (Luke 14:26). Paul tells us that our affections are to be set on things above (Col. 3:1).

We are not what Christ would have us to be. If this is the measure of the Christian life, if this is what God desires of us as Christians, like Isaiah we must cry, "Woe is me, for I am undone!"

Why did not the Lord Jesus Christ, who is so tender and so understanding, so loving and so wise, make requirements of us more in keeping with our human frailties? Why does He not demand of us what we might reasonably attain? He bids us soar, yet we have no wings. It is not natural for us to love our enemies. It is not natural to rejoice always. It is not natural to be thankful for things that hurt. It is not natural to hate ourselves. It is not natural to walk as Jesus walked.

This is no new dilemma. Paul makes no bones about his conviction that human nature can never attain the high calling of Christ. He lets the glaring fact of Christ's law as an utterly unattainable ideal stand out in all its naked reality. Romans 7 is witness to that fact. Here is Paul's final confession of failure, his cry of despair, his bitter regret upon finding the Christian ideal absolutely unattainable.

I quote Paul's own words:

> *The good that I will to do, I do not do; but the evil which I will not to do, that I do. . .I delight in the law of God according to the inward man, but I see another law in my members (there's the rub) warring against the law of my mind, and bringing me into captivity to the law of sin which is in my members. Oh, wretched man that I am! Who will deliver me from this body of death?*
>
> *(Rom. 7:19-24)*

Paul struggles. He agonizes. He weeps. He strives as only this spiritual giant could. The result? It all comes to no avail! The law of sin, Paul confesses, like the onrush of a mighty stream, sweeps everything before it .

Your efforts to be a good Christian will win no better results! You will do well to face squarely all the shocking aspects of this dilemma. Paul did. He candidly acknowledges that he delights in God's law, loves it, but finds it something to which human nature cannot attain. If you will be honest about these things, you will take certain steps which will lead you into a glorious new day.

It was not that Paul, when he wrote Romans 7, was still willfully disobedient, as in the days prior to his Damascus road crisis. He loved Jesus. He was a soldier of the Cross. He was a consecrated Christian. It was only that he was now seeing himself in a new light—in the blinding light of the Cross of Christ! Now his failures are repulsive to him. They are unbearable. They seem to burn with the fire of hell. They sting like the bite of a scorpion. They break his heart.

It is no longer a question of mere ethics, of right or wrong. Paul wants to be free to be like Jesus in all the loveliness of His humility and compassion. He desires to love God with a pure love and serve Him with that utter singleness of eye which characterized Jesus. In a paroxysm of self-loathing, and in the anguish of self-despair, the apostle cries out for deliverance (Rom. 7:24).

Is there a way out? Yes, Paul found it, and you can find it. I say that we have been proceeding upon a false basis. You have conceived of the Christian life as an *imitation* of Christ. It is not an imitation of Christ, it is a *participation in* Christ.

For we have become partakers *of Christ.*

(Heb. 3:14)

There are good things in Thomas a Kempis' *Imitation of Christ,* but the basic idea is false to the principles that underlie the Christian life. To proceed on the basis of imitation will plunge you into the "slough of despond" exactly like the one

Paul found himself in, which he recorded in Romans 7.

So you are not what Christ would have you to be: There is little joy, so little freedom of spirit, none of that rapture which so characterized the early Christians; there is agony and struggle. Failure dogs your every footstep. What is the matter? You are proceeding on a false basis. You are attempting to do what the Savior Himself never expected you to do. The Christian life is not a life of imitation!

The great dilemma of which we have been speaking resolves itself into the most simple terms when we grasp the distinction between imitation and participation.

What is impossible to you as an *imitator* of Christ becomes perfectly natural as a *participant* of Christ. Christ nullifies the forces of your fallen human life, and then communicates to you a divine life. That life does the Christian living. And that life became available to you when you were born again.

Without Jesus' unique life doing it all, I can do nothing. I must live in Him and find in Him a new life.

The Christian requirements are all simple for this new life to do. These are its *modus operandi*, its functioning principles. The Sermon on the Mount does not cramp this new life—it is the way this heavenly life operates.

Jesus tells us that we must abide in Him as a branch in the Vine. The moral mandates of Matthew 5, 6, 7, without the Vine-branch relationship spoken of in John 15 would be like so many freight cars without an engine, like a whale without water, or a bird without air.

In that upper-room interview, Christ places supreme

emphasis upon this mystical oneness—this spiritual oneness of Himself with all believers. His spirit and your spirit. . . one . . .is this sublime fact of participation. "Abide in Me, and I in you."

Our failures only confirm the Savior's words, for He said, "Without Me you can do nothing."

No, we are not called upon to imitate Christ. The truth of the matter is, there would be little virtue in doing so. Paul said so, in effect, in his oft-quoted "love-chapter" (1 Cor. 13.) It could only be a wooden, artificial thing.

Some years ago in the country where I was serving in the Lord's vineyard, this sort of thing was carried to its nth degree when a zealous devotee had himself crucified, *literally* nailed to a cross. That is where his parents found him dead. The church rightly does not accept that sort of thing, yet vast multitudes in the church proceed theoretically on the false basis of imitation.

No Christian is called upon to strain as an actor might agonize over his role in a play. The Christian life, in the thought of God, is infinitely more blessed and compelling.

We have *become partakers of Christ.*

(Heb. 3:14)

Exceedingly great and precious promises are given to us "that through these we may be partakers of the divine nature" (2 Peter 1:4).

The believer is grafted into the trunk of the Eternal Godhead. "I am the Vine, you are the branches."

> . . .the riches of the glory of this mystery
> . . .Christ in you, the hope of glory!
>
> *(Col. 1:27)*

2

Christ's Death Our Death

See the length and breadth, the depth and height, of this marvelous identification you have with your Savior.

Christ and all true believers are one. They constitute His body. They are, in the language of Paul, "members of His body, of His flesh and of His bones" (Eph. 5:30).

We are bone of his bone. It is but *one* bone. Just what the implications of this oneness with Christ are—and the overwhelming glory of such a position—most Christians do not even have an inkling.

Your oneness with Christ is the only spring that can quench your thirst. There is no other way to fulfillment of your deepest aspirations as a Christian.

It is the business of the Holy Spirit to graft you into Christ, even as a gardener would graft the branch of a tree into the trunk of another.

By one Spirit we were all baptized into one body.

(1 Cor. 12:13)

In the eleventh chapter of Paul's letter to the Romans, he speaks of the breaking off of Israel from the Root, Christ, and the grafting in of the Gentiles to become partakers of the Root. You are rooted into the very trunk of the eternal Godhead.

Do not simply strive to imitate a divine leader. You are made a partaker of the divine nature (2 Peter 1:4)! And the Spirit Himself bears witness with your spirit that you are a child of God, an heir of God, and joint heir with Christ (Rom. 8:16-17).

It was the Spirit who revealed Christ to you as the only way out—your sin bearer, your salvation (John 16: 7-15). It is the same Spirit who binds you to Christ, rooting your life into His divine life, causing you to grow up into Him who is the Head.

He has become your life; you believed *into* Christ.

He who is joined to the Lord is one spirit with Him.

(1 Cor. 6:17)

Now this grafting necessitates some cutting, of course. If you will not die to the natural, how can you expect to live to the supernatural? Paul puts it this way:

If we be dead with Christ, we believe that we shall also live with Him.

(Rom. 6:8)

The branch which, contrary to nature, is grafted into a tree of another species must die to the old life. It must send its roots into a new trunk, and so it receives a new life. Its relation with the old original tree is severed utterly, completely and continuously.

The Holy Spirit works in you conviction of the sin of a divided heart. He shows you how tragically self-will has thwarted Christ's purpose to bring you into utter union with Himself. He reveals, with racking precision and crushing clearness, the awful consequences of living the fallen human life, in its enmity to Christ and its power to choke the life of your spirit. He shows you the duplicity of your way, the shamefulness of a hollow piety, the mockery of a superficial devotion to Christ. You begin to see that though you have been rooted into Christ, yet you have been drawing more from the old roots. You see how muddy is the stream of your life, how tainted the waters, how the stench of your fallen life has blighted the flowers that have grown alongside. You begin to understand Romans 7. The secret cry of your heart becomes: "O wretched man that I am! Who will deliver me from this body of death?"

This marks a crisis. The hour has come for a fresh revelation of Christ's redemptive work. Your eyes are now to be opened to the meaning of the deeper aspects of the Cross of Christ.

The Cross is now unveiled. The Holy Spirit reveals Christ—this time not as the divine Sin Bearer, but as the way out of this loathsome thing we call self and the self-life. You

are given a vision of yourself as one with Christ in His death
. . .crucified with Christ. You are made to see that you too
died to sin, in the death of the Savior.

You realize that if you fail to sign the death sentence of
self, your position as a believer becomes utterly intolerable,
the acme of contradictions.

You begin to realize that Christ not only died for you as a
sinner, but that you died in Christ to sin. You know you must
either die with Christ to sin or continue to crucify Christ. You
see that unless self is crucified, Christ is.

It is all the work of the Holy Spirit. It is not natural for
you to turn against yourself and to begin to hate that which by
nature you love as nothing else under the sun—that is, your
self.

The Holy Spirit—writes Dr. A. B. Simpson in *Days of
Heaven*—is the great Undertaker who finally brings us to the
place to which God has assigned us: to a sharing of Christ's
tomb. But He cannot bring you to this participation in
crucifixion-life—to the place called Calvary—without your
consent. You must consent to die.

The Cross signifies pain and shame, ignominy and
death—the breaking of the heart of Christ. All this was not
too much for the Savior, if He could but woo you from yourself
and get your consent to die. That is why the Cross saves. It
is not achieved by divine magic. The purpose of Calvary strikes
infinitely deeper than that.

If you have looked to the Lamb of God who takes away
the sin of the world without a profound willingness to be

unhinged from the false center, your fallen self, then it is safe to say that the fullest purpose of God simply has not been attained. The Holy Spirit has never had a chance to work in you so as to bring you to a spiritual participation in the death of the Son of God—which in the divine economy was corporate. Christ's redeemed body, the church, died in its divine head.

Paul saw this so clearly that he cries out as if stabbed when the startling thought of a possible continuance in sin, after having come to faith in Christ, is suggested. "What! Shall we continue in sin that grace may abound?" Well, why not if, after all, salvation, as so many are accustomed to think of it, is simply a release from the penal consequences of sin. Ah! Says the apostle:

> *How shall we who died to sin live any longer in it? Or do you not know that as many of us as were baptized into Jesus Christ were baptized into His death?. . .We were buried with Him. . .into death. . .We have been united together in the likeness of His death. . .Our old man was crucified with Him, that the body of sin might be done away with. . .The death that (Christ) died, He died to sin once for all . . .Likewise you also, reckon yourselves to be dead indeed to sin, but alive to God in Christ Jesus our Lord.*
>
> *(Rom. 6:1-11)*

Truth out of proportion, it has been fitly said, becomes error. The truth of Christ's substitutionary death without your participation in the Cross (your willingness to have the Spirit detach you from self and center you in God) will put you into the confusion which error always brings about.

In the memoirs of Mrs. Penn-Lewis there is a strange story, connected with her visit to India, which fits most beautifully into this line of thought. There was a missionary who later gave himself with the zeal of an apostle to the task of propagating the writings of Mrs. Penn-Lewis, which almost all bear upon the believer's identification with Christ in death and resurrection. This missionary had a dream that greatly impressed him. It was of the Cross of Christ. It was not the Savior's bleeding form which held his eye. It was an exceedingly ugly thing, an indescribably loathsome thing, the nature of which he could not make out. What was this thing which so horrified him? Later, as he heard the message of identification and realized that with Christ he had been crucified, the Spirit revealed to him that this loathsome thing he had seen in his dream was none other than himself.

The very nature of "self" is such that misery must follow in its wake.

Christ's object was to terminate the "old creation," taking you down into the grave, putting an end to your old life, and then bring you forth in resurrection power charged with the dynamic of a heavenly life! Speaking of Jew and Gentile, Paul says:

(Christil). . .having abolished in His flesh the
enmity. . .so as to create in Himself one new
man from the two. . .through the Cross.

(Eph. 2:15-16)

New. . .in Him. . .what a spiritual revolution it would work
in the life of the church! A tidal wave of divine life would
sweep through her, revitalizing the members of Christ's body
(so many of whom are languishing in the swamps of spiritual
decrepitude) giving them a fresh joy, and firing them with
heavenly Life.

The church, as has said the great French preacher
Lacordaire, was born crucified; and until, like her divine head,
she falls into the ground and dies, she abides alone. The life-
giving streams cannot break forth from her bosom.

God grant you the grace to be clear about one thing: Christ
does not come into your life to patch up your "old man." Here
is where unnumbered multitudes of Christians have been "hung
up." They thought it was Christ's mission to make them better.
There is absolutely no biblical ground for any such idea. Jesus
said that He had no intention of pouring His new wine into
old pigskins. He said that He had not come to bring peace,
but a sword. He said that unless a man would renounce himself
utterly, he could not be His disciple.

Christ does not come to you to simply straighten out your
"old life." He has never promised to make us better. His
entire redemptive work which was consummated upon the

Cross rests upon the assumption (it is more than an assumption—God says it is a fact) that man's condition is such that only dying and being born again can possibly make any change in you. He must impart to you an entirely new life.

Christ is the Vine, we are the branches. He is the Head, we form the Body.

Paul's epistles again and again point us to Calvary and startle us with an imperative demand: We must consent to co-crucifixion with Christ.

I have often wondered about that symbolic standard which Moses lifted up in the desert, and to which our Lord referred in the classic interview with Nicodemus, when He said: "As Moses lifted up the serpent in the wilderness, even so must the Son of Man be lifted up." I have wondered why it had to be a serpent. Why not something lovely, inasmuch as it was to typify the King in His redemptive work upon the Cross? We read that all who looked to the serpent were healed. But why a serpent? Why not a lily, or a rose? Was it not the Rose of Sharon who was thus represented?

It was only after I had discovered this principle of *identification with Christ* that I came to understand. Christ was not there on Calvary's cross alone. Our "old self" was being crucified in the Second Adam—Christ the Representative Man—who was there upon the accursed tree not for Himself, but for mankind: there as one so identified with suffering, sinning man, so merged with the human race in its iniquity and its depravity, that He could not die for sin and to sin unless man should die in Him. Since my accursed, loathsome "self-life" (fallen life) was nailed there to the Cross with Christ, and in the judgment of God died in Him, what more fitting symbol than the serpent?

Your self-life has poisoned the very springs of your being, such as a dreaded disease might do.

Not long ago, I was reading about the strange lot of certain young ladies who are employed in a laboratory where contact with radium is inevitable. These young ladies know that upon entering this factory their fate is sealed. They will die. After a few months or years—I do not recall the exact time—they are released from their work with a handsome check for thousands of dollars. Some live a year, some two, some three, but all eventually die from the effects of radiation; hence the ample remuneration. Doctors have examined girls who have worked in contact with radium, and have found by means of the x-ray that a strange fire, slowly consuming the life, is burning in their bones. Radiation kills.

Two thousand years ago, there in the manger of Bethlehem, God gave to the world His only-begotten Son. In Him was concentrated the infinite love of the Father. But the full force of that redeeming love was not released upon a sin-stricken world until there on Calvary the flaming heart of the Beloved broke. Then it was that the radium of the celestial realm was focused upon the great cancer of humanity's sin and shame. Radiation kills. There is no power under heaven that can withstand its concentrated dynamic.

The Cross also kills. The man who exposes himself to Calvary soon discovers that a hidden fire burns within his bones.

The old fallen life—so resentful, so fussy, so greedy, so touchy, so haughty, so vain, so blind to all except its own particular lust, so ready to sacrifice the good of the many if only its own glory may be secured—the old "self-life" can no more resist the impact of Calvary than can some frail canoe survive the onrush of a great tidal wave.

Dr. Mabie, in his notable work *The Cross,* speaks of the Savior's death as "immortal-dying." It was not mere dying. The rocks were rent, and the earth quaked when in that hour of triumph the Son of Man cried out with a loud voice, "It is finished!" Life did not merely ebb out. The force of it increased. That is why in the final hour the great cry of consummation shook the very earth. "When the centurion, who stood opposite Him, saw that He cried out *like this*. . .he said, 'Truly this Man was the Son of God!'" (Mark 15:39). The "old-life," brought under the dynamic of the Cross, is doomed to die. Resurrection life takes its place. Little wonder the apostle to the Gentiles cried out, "God forbid that I should glory except in the Cross of our Lord Jesus Christ, by whom the world has been crucified to me, and I to the world."

"We preach Christ crucified, to the Jews a stumbling block and to the Greeks foolishness, but to those who are called, both Jews and Greeks, Christ the power of God." (Power, in Greek, is *dunamis,* from which we get our word dynamite.)

The full meaning of your identification with the Savior in His death cannot be taken in at a glance. No scriptural truth which has to do with your Christian life can be really yours until it has worked within you. As Christians we cannot speak of possessing truth apart from Him who is Truth.

Mature Christians who have experienced an inner crucifixion and who know what it means to count upon Christ's death may have thought that they were wholly the Lord's and the old self was buried with Christ; then some hidden shifting of the scenes seems to awaken the old life and to set in motion the secret workings of the self-life. They come to realize their need for a fresh and deeper experience of the Cross.

Their only way out is through a renewed participation in Christ's death. Only the radium of Calvary can remove the remaining roots of the old cancer. They rise, so to speak, to higher heights of spiritual life by sinking themselves into deeper depths of death. However deep they may have gone, Calvary has for them still undreamed-of depths of crucifixion.

Let us further examine this matter of identification with Christ. It is both a *position* which you take once and for all by an act of faith (in which you commit yourself to your place in the death of His Son) and a *process of growth*, in which you receive an ever-deepening life of sharing in the Savior's death. Even Paul said that he longed to know Christ and the power of His resurrection. . .being made conformable unto His death (Phil. 3:10). It is all summed up in the great paradox of the gospel: "He who loses his life shall find it."

There is not any nullification of personality involved. Quite the contrary. Paul was no less Paul after the realization of his oneness with Christ in death. He could, with infinitely more right, say "Nevertheless I live." Once the Cross deals with the "I-life" so that the soul becomes God-centered, personality in all of its glory and the full fruition of its powers begins to develop. You can only possess yourself when God is supreme in your life.

The Savior's substitutionary death for you became effective in the blotting out of your sins upon the exercise of faith. Even so your participation in Christ's death becomes effective upon the exercise of faith. Being born again you might call a participation in the legal benefits of Christ's redemptive work; being one with Christ's death may be called participating in the life-changing aspect of the work of the Cross. Your willingness is the supreme condition in receiving either, though we do violence to the spirit of the Cross if we separate the two realities. They are meant to be one.

When I say your willingness is the prime condition, I mean that God cannot when you will not. He can only work these mighty works in your life, upon the condition of your consent. Done on any other basis, they could have no meaning. In the act of creation, by giving you freedom of will, God limited Himself. Moved by infinite love, He shared with you His very divinity, setting bounds to His own omnipotence by endowing you with the power to choose. God never has and never will violate that freedom. God woos you, but never forces you. He appeals in a thousand ways to the best in you, but never coerces you. He pleads with you, shows you the terrible consequences of sin (witness the Cross), but He never forces you to come back into loving relations with Himself.

So you must choose. Will you be dominated by self or Christ? Will you continue to pamper self and crucify Christ afresh, or will you die to the self-life (call it what you will, flesh-life, the old life, the carnal—it matters not) and rise up out of that grave to begin to live in the power of Christ's resurrection? This is the great issue which the Cross of Christ raises.

Could the wisdom of the ages conceive a more potent way—a more irresistible way—a surer way of obtaining man's consent to be detached from self? If anything better designed to give man a loathing for self and a love for God could be found, we may be sure that God would have produced it. "Christ crucified" is truly "the power of God and the wisdom of God" (1Cor. 1:23-24).

"Our old man was crucified with Christ." Some versions say "*is* crucified." It is true both ways. We can neither add nor subtract from a divinely finished work.

Being in Christ, we are crucified. Your being a German or a Frenchman makes inevitable certain habits of mind, a certain temperament of soul. Your being a Christian makes inevitable a crucified life. The church did not come forth from the womb of the Eternal until, upon the Cross, crucified life had been generated.

For this purpose Jesus came. His death was no mere accident. He was "slain from the foundation of the world." His death was not simply that of a martyr. He said:

I lay down My life that I may take it again.
No one takes it from Me, but I lay it down of
Myself.   *(John 10:17-18)*

31

But for this purpose I came to this hour.

(John 12:27)

Truly, His death was no afterthought, but the necessary basis for the building of a crucified church. He became a crucified Christ that He might have crucified followers.

But, I repeat, you must choose—choose what is already potentially your position before God. On the basis of the Cross, and your oneness with Christ in death, you choose to refuse the old life.

The kingdom of heaven suffers violence, and the violent (those who are bold and determined) take it by force.

(Matt. 11:12)

You must not only refuse the old life in a sublime moment of surrender, but you do it consistently, every time your fallen nature would reinstate itself. You do it as consistently and as habitually as you would hold your nose from the stench of some filthy alley which you might pass. As a free moral agent, you choose, and choose again, and again, and continue to choose.

Which will you have? The divine life which flows as a great river of life from the throne of God and the Lamb? Then you must refuse your fallen life. It has been corrupted by sin. Cut yourself off from it by standing in Christ's death! Receive a heavenly life moment by moment. Do this, and you shall be more than a conqueror. Do this, and you will no longer agonize over seeking to imitate Christ. You could not be anything but like Him, sharing as you do His death and His resurrection. It will be an easy thing, a joyous thing, a lovely thing—like the play of children. It is now natural for you to be a Christian, for you have been made a partaker of the divine nature.

The church has been enjoying a fifty percent redemption because she has not realized all the implications of the Cross. She has not been willing to die with her Lord because she has not believed her Lord. She has tried to imitate her Lord, in the energy of the old life, in order to reproduce His way. She has not been willing to acknowledge her utter inability to do this, or willing to lay down her life in order to share His heavenly life.

A deep eternal union, a grafting of the soul into Christ, a great merging of interests, purposes, aspirations—all to be consummated. This is the gospel. But God, in terms so unmistakable that all ages, all races, and all generations may grasp the meaning, has revealed the basis on which this union may be achieved. It is through the Cross of Christ.

It is interesting to note how that in the great book of nature this same lesson is taught—that all life springs out of death. Not a tree, not a blossom, not a shrub, not a fruit, but what costs the death of a seed.

The other day a cotton planter took me out to see his

plantation. I am so glad that he insisted that I follow him out between the rows of cotton, for God spoke to me through my friend's exposition of the ways of cottonseed. He dug up half a dozen seeds—just sprouting—to show me, in a manner I can never forget, that before the seed sends any sprouts up it sends a long root down. One would imagine that the seed already buried would have enough of death, and that it would send its first sprout up for air and light and freedom. No, first down deeper in its already-hidden tomb.

How clearly, through the Old Testament type and symbol and story, the Holy Spirit flashes light upon this mystery— this fact of our co-crucifixion with Christ. Here are some examples:

Abraham must sacrifice his Isaac. Isaac was spared, yet in spirit Abraham offered him up. It was because he had done this thing that the promise was made: "In blessing I will bless you, and in multiplying I will multiply your descendants as the stars of the heaven and as the sand which is on the seashore." And even previous to that, we read that it was from "the womb as good as dead" that his son had issued.

Joseph is buried in an Egyptian prison before he rises to become a veritable savior, seated on the throne which he seemed to share with the mighty Pharaoh.

For forty years on the lonely slopes of Midian the fiery Moses is schooled. There were graves, if I may so speak, scattered all over the mountainside where hope after hope was buried until at last self went down in utter annihilation. Except for those graves, the man of God who became the moral giant of antiquity, who spoke face to face with Jehovah, and whose guiding hand will be felt in the affairs of nations until the end of time, could not have been.

If Leviticus with its myriad sacrifices, its rivers of blood, means anything, it means that God meets man on but one basis—the basis of the Cross.

Our pleasure-infatuated age will stop its ears and gnash its teeth as did those who stoned Stephen. For these things hurt. But if you have tasted of the Lord, if you pant after the wine of heaven, if you cannot be satisfied with anything short of the fullness of the Spirit, and if your heart is "a furnace of desire" for the deep things of God—then these truths that cut and burn, and blast away the old life, will be welcomed with an unspeakable joy.

The Israelites must go down into the valley of the Jordan, leaving in the bed of the stream twelve stones, in order to enter the land of milk and honey. The waters return as Israel passes, burying the twelve stones, symbolic of Israel's twelve tribes. Israel cannot abide in Canaan without a constant abiding in death through the twelve symbolic stones, buried in the stream (Josh 4:9).

David does not come to the throne until in the caves of the Philistines, where he was hunted down like a dog by the infuriated Saul, he dies deaths innumerable. The psalms, with all their varied loveliness, so adapted to human woe, their seraphic unfolding of the life of communion, could not have come about, except for the inner crucifixion in the heart of the sweet singer of Israel brought about by the mad persecutions of Saul.

35

Isaiah sees the Lord and is undone. He must be purged of the old life by a fiery coal from off the altar of heaven.

Jeremiah dies a thousand deaths as he weeps over the unrepentant chosen people.

Jonah is pitched into the sea and is swallowed by a whale— yet even then he does not come forth wholly purged from self.

God's people have never in any age come to the mountain peak of spiritual attainment, the glory of unbroken communion with the Most High, without having the self-life, the flesh-life, brought again and again to the dust of death.

When the "fair one" of Canticles cries out, "Let him kiss me with the kisses of his mouth" (the symbolical language of the soul's thirst for union with Christ), speedily there follows the confession: "A bundle of myrrh (bitterness) is my beloved to me. . .My beloved is to me a cluster of henna blooms (cemetery-tree flowers) in the vineyards of En Gedi." Ah yes, it must be death! The Beloved cannot bring us to union with Himself without a deep participation in His Cross.

Have you taken your place with Christ in His death? By an act of faith you must lay hold of that death as your death. Take your stand with Christ on Calvary ground, and each time the self-life would assert itself, say, "In Christ I died; in His name I refuse." This done, the Holy Spirit will bear witness to your faith and set you free, and keep you free.

3

Co-Crucifixion With Christ

Though the apostle Paul never knew Christ while He was on earth, he seems to have had a deeper insight into the mysteries of the faith than the other apostles had. After Jesus Christ, he is the outstanding personality of the New Testament, making the greatest contribution to the literature and the growth of the church, even though he had never come under the sway of the Savior's earthly teaching and ministry.

After the Damascus Road revelation, Paul did not head to Jerusalem "to confer with flesh and blood." He went to Arabia. He wanted to be alone. Such an experience as he had had—the vision of blinding light, the sudden appearance of ineffable glory, the discovery that the Jesus of the accursed tree was the Christ of God—such an overwhelming revelation of the power and beauty of Him who is the King of kings made a period of silence and rapt meditation absolutely imperative (Gal. 1:16-18).

It would seem as though he was making a great mistake!

What? Not go to Jerusalem to consult with Peter, James and John? Think of it, Paul who had never known Jesus could have sat at the feet of the apostles! He could have talked it all over with Peter. He could have obtained first-hand information from John. Some of us would have traveled around the world for such a privilege. Did Paul make a mistake? We will let Paul speak for himself:

> *When it pleased God. . .to reveal His Son in*
> *me. . .I did not immediately confer with flesh*
> *and blood, nor did I go up to Jerusalem to*
> *those who were apostles before me; but I went*
> *to Arabia. . .*
>
> *(Gal.1:15-17)*

Christ filled and flooded his horizon. The glory of Christ so absorbed him that for three years he could not detach himself from the heavenly magnet.

Fourteen years later he again went up to Jerusalem, but he made the significant confession that those who were reputed to be something added nothing to him (Gal.2:6). The apostles could give him no light. The contrary was the case: Paul understood better; he had more light. He knew Christ better. His insight into such questions as the relation of the Gentiles to the church, the relation of Christianity to Judaism, the reality of the indwelling Christ, of the mystical "body," the understanding of justification by faith, the universality of Christianity—his insight into the mysteries of the faith was deeper. His judgment was sounder.

The three years in the Arabian desert at the feet of the glorified Christ had done infinitely more for this once-proud Pharisee than the three years with the man Jesus had done for the fishermen apostles. Paul was always ahead of them. After our Lord, it is to Paul that the church owes the greatest debt.

Now how do we account for this? Paul, who had never known Jesus after the flesh, knew Him better after the Spirit. He, as none other, was hid with Christ in God. He had been caught up to the third heaven where he heard inexpressible things, things that man is not permitted to tell. It was he who prayed for his Ephesian brethren that the Lord would strengthen them with might by His Spirit in the inner man; that Christ might dwell in their hearts by faith; that they, rooted and grounded in love, might be able to comprehend with all saints what is the length and breadth and depth and height, and to know the love of Christ which surpasses knowledge, and that they might be filled with all the fullness of God.

The great apostle's glorying was not simply in the fact that Christ had died for him. Along with that, there was always associated another aspect of the Cross, namely, the fact that he (Paul) had died in Christ.

> *God forbid that I should glory except in the Cross of our Lord Jesus Christ, by whom the world has been crucified to me, and I to the world.*
>
> *(Gal.6:14)*

Our old man was crucified with Him, that the body of sin might be done away with.

(Rom. 6:6)

Shall we continue in sin that grace may abound? Certainly not! How shall we who died to sin live any longer in it?

(Rom. 6:1-2)

For you died, and your life is hidden with Christ in God.

(Col. 3:3)

This seems to be the sublime lesson which the Savior burned into the fiber of Paul's being, there in the Arabian desert where he listened in rapt wonderment. It was the deep meaning of Calvary which the Lord unfolded to the now-broken Pharisee—to him who was to become the greatest of the apostles. The veil was drawn aside and Paul gazed into the hidden mysteries of the Cross. He saw himself there with Jesus, potentially crucified. For Paul, the Christian life was never to be a mere imitation, but a glorious participation in the Savior's death and resurrection. For him, the believer was a member of Christ's body—bone of His bone, and flesh of His flesh. For him, to live was Christ. He would not have some of self and some of Christ, nor even a little of self and much of Christ. He simply would have none of self, and all of Christ. He saw that God had laid not only sins but also the sinner upon the Cross, and that in Christ he, Paul, had died. He never wavered. He committed the self-life to death and stood forth before the world, free in Christ.

So the great apostle utterly identifies himself with Christ. The apostle identifies himself so utterly with his Lord and Savior Jesus Christ that he sees in his own sufferings as a follower of Christ what we may call a continuation of Calvary. Paul speaks of it as a completing of what was lacking in the afflictions of Christ. In a word, the apostle interprets his own sufferings in the light of the Cross.

We see this in the second Corinthian letter where he dwells upon the persecutions and trials which he bore. "We are hard pressed on every side," he says, "perplexed. . .persecuted. . . struck down." Then follows the amazing utterance which gives us the key for the interpretation of the deepest secret of Paul's innermost soul: "always carrying about in the body the dying of the Lord Jesus. . . ." It is Christ suffering, it is Christ receiving fresh wounds, it is Christ being crucified afresh in and through His servant. Paul sees in the Cross not only the death of the Savior, but also the potential death of all those who constitute His body. This reality is so complete that he sees his own sufferings and the sufferings of all Christians as a filling up of that which is lacking in regard to Christ's afflictions (Col. 1:24).

But do not think of this death as something purely negative.

From this death springs life—eternal life!

> *Always carrying about in the body the dying*
> *of the Lord Jesus, that the life of Jesus also*
> *may be manifested in our body. . . .So then*
> *death is working in us, but life in you.*
>
> *(2 Cor. 4:10-12)*

It is when you die in Christ to the old life that the barriers are all removed and the living streams break forth from your innermost being, bearing the life of God to others.

Before we leave this phase of our being in Christ, let us briefly summarize what we have seen in Paul's writings.

First, in Christ we are dead to sin (Rom. 6:11). Sin is not overcome simply by struggling against it. If it were only something which always met us from without, that might not be so difficult. But our very being is soaked with it. A drop of ink in a glass of water will taint the entire glass. No amount of patchwork, no mere polishing or varnish will do. Jesus says we must be born again. So in Christ we are taken into the tomb to be undone.

Second, in Christ we are dead to the world. That does not mean that a monastery or a desert retreat would be more conducive to Christian living. No man ever stood nearer the heart of this world's affairs than Christ, whether in the marketplace, in the home, in the temple, with the poor, the maimed, the blind, or with those who rejoiced at a bridal feast. He was ever in the stream of life where the current was swiftest and deepest. He was not an ascetic. Yet He could say, "I am not of the world." And, "They are not of the world, just as I am not of the world."

The world has taken on plenty of gloss since Christ's day, but friendship with the world is still enmity with God. Be on intimate terms with this world which crucified Christ? It is unthinkable. We are dead to the world in Christ (Gal. 6:14).

In the third place, in Christ we die to any party spirit. Paul, speaking in his Ephesian letter of the middle wall between Jews and Gentiles, says that Christ broke down this wall by His Cross, "creating in Himself one new man from the two." If the church could see herself crucified with Christ, the walls would break down. The wall, for example, of sectarianism. "In Christ there is neither Jew nor Greek." Any intense holding of sectarian attitudes is positively unchristian. All division is of the flesh. Satan raises walls between person and person, group and group, denomination and denomination, nation and nation. Christ breaks them down.

Christ. . .is our peace, who has made both one,
and has broken down the middle wall of
division between us, having abolished in His
flesh the enmity. . .so as to create in Himself
one new man from the two (Jew and Gentile),
thus making peace. . . that He might reconcile
them both to God in one body through the

Cross, thereby putting to death the enmity.
(Eph. 2:13-16)

Finally, in Christ we have died to the law.

My brethren, you also have become dead to
the law through the body of Christ.

(Rom. 7:4)

Christ has lifted you not only out of the flesh-life and cut you off from the world by His death in which you participate, but has taken you clear out of the realm of law. You are not under the law but under grace—for it is the law of the Spirit of life in Christ Jesus which governs you. In a sense it is still law, "the perfect law of liberty," of which James speaks in his epistle. But do not confuse this with the Law of Moses. The one liberates; the other binds. The one gives the power to be Christlike; the other is dead legalism. The one is an expression of the new nature; the other is an attempt to check and control the old nature.

How good it is to be free—free from the dominion of the fallen life, free from the tyranny of the world, free from the monster which we call self. Free also from the legalism of a dead law which, as Paul says, works wrath. Free from the bondage of fear and anxiety and worry. How good to have a liberated spirit surcharged with the life of God! It is the Cross of Christ that liberates. Only as you stand with Christ in His death and receive by faith the liberating force of Calvary can you hope to experience the true freedom for which your spirit pants.

4

Participating in Christ's Resurrection

As we go forward step by step, considering your participation in Christ, you will find that it is the key to unfathomable riches, the Aladdin's Lamp of unspeakable power, the gateway to such happiness as you had never dreamed could be possible this side of the gates of heaven.

You cannot take these steps without experiencing such a radical revolution in your attitudes, your relationships and your thinking that all things indeed become new. You look back upon the old way of imitation, struggle, failure, confusion—the old way of living from your fallen life—and you feel unutterable relief, unspeakable gratitude that a new day has dawned. No disinherited prince who, after years of strife has at last come to his own name, his own wealth, his own power in his father's palace, could look back upon his years of loss and shame with feelings any more profound.

You find that after yielding all to the Lord, He comes so to possess you by His Spirit that your very frame of mind is governed by Him. Are you moved to pray? He gives you a spirit of prayer; He gives you access into the presence of the living God. And your prayers have a force and a vitality that lead you to laugh at the impossible. Are you tried? He holds you in His bosom and the kisses of His mouth make your heart sing. Are you tempted? He girds you with might. You are more than conqueror in Him.

The next step which we would consider is our participation in Christ's resurrection. Not only did you die in Christ—in Him you arose. Your death to self is but the gateway to a larger, fuller life—the more abundant life. As you sign your death warrant and consign the old life to the grave, it is only to find that you are the recipient of a life infinitely more wonderful — divine life, eternal life.

> *God, who is rich in mercy, because of His great love with which He loved us. . .has made us alive together with Christ. . .and has raised us up together.*
>
> *(Eph. 2:4-6)*

Marvelous truth! Glorious fact! How it enriches! What treasure of grace, what power, what glory — what a wealth of meaning! Christ's resurrection *your* resurrection. God raised you up together with Him. He is sufficient for your deepest need. "As the deer pants for the water brooks, so pants my soul for You, O God."

Jesus said that such a life was to be at the disposal of the believer. "Whoever drinks of this water will thirst again, but whoever drinks of the water that I shall give him will never thirst. But the water that I shall give him will become in him a fountain of water springing up into everlasting life." "He who believes in Me, out of his heart will flow rivers of living water." "I have come that they may have life, and that they may have it more abundantly." "I am the bread of life. He who comes to Me shall never hunger, and he who believes in Me shall never thirst."

In some measure, all believers enjoy this divine life, even those still dominated by the fallen life. For some it is a tiny rivulet almost imperceptible, for others it is as a mighty stream, rivers of living water—the degree being determined by the degree of union with Christ and dependence upon Him. (See Ezekiel 47, the vision of the rising waters.) Were this divine life not something which in a measure all believers receive, you could not participate in Christ's cross. Only a living creature can die; and so, only souls that have in a measure received the Christ-life can die to self.

Self cannot overcome self. You must be Christ-possessed to die to the self-life. And to the degree in which you receive Christ, you die to self.

In the first chapter of the Ephesian letter, Paul utters a marvelous prayer. He says to the Ephesians:

I do not cease to give thanks for you, making
mention of you in my prayers: that the God of

our Lord Jesus Christ, the Father of glory, may
give to you the spirit of wisdom and revelation
in the knowledge of Him, the eyes of your
understanding being enlightened; that you
may know. . .what is the exceeding greatness
of His power toward us who believe.

And this power which is *to* us, *for* us, *in* us who believe—
from where does it come? What actually is it? It is the "power
which [God] worked in Christ when He *raised Him from the
dead.*"

That is the matchless power which works in you—the
power of Christ's resurrection! Paul longed to have the
Ephesians realize that fact.

When we come to consider the requirements of the New
Testament as they bear upon the Christian life, we realize that
they all presuppose this very oneness of the believer with Christ
in the power of His resurrection. No one but a Christ-centered
person, one with Him in death and resurrection, could possibly
measure up to the ideal of Christ in Christian life and service.
To love one's enemies with that divine love (Greek *agape*,
divine-type love) without a deep participation in the power of
Christ's endless life would no more be possible for the purely
natural man than for a worm to play the role of a bird. There
is not a New Testament requirement that does not immediately
bring you face to face with an overwhelming dilemma. Either
you must cease to move in the realm of the purely natural—

find in the resurrected Christ a new life—or you must fail as a Christian. To the new life—the life that flows from Christ—the Sermon on the Mount presents no problems; it is all natural, easy, a spontaneous expression of principles already inherent. The ways, customs, language of jungle savages are no more unintelligible or impracticable to the average person today than is the Sermon on the Mount to one who has not been born again (i.e., died to the self-life to rise up with Christ in the power of a new life).

A mere mechanical doing-as-Jesus-did will never bring you to the Christ-life. For a dead frog can be made to kick as if it were alive by the touch of an electric current, but it remains dead. Nor can my imitation of the ways of a Frenchman make me a Frenchman. I am an American, and I would have to be reborn to be anything but what I am.

You had to be born anew. That is why Christ took you with Himself down into the grave and brought you forth a new creation. He terminated your old life when there upon the Cross as Representative Man He died; and He imparted to you a new life when He arose from the grave.

Christ expects nothing from your flesh. However religious its garments, however holy its appearance, however sanctified its undertakings, it still "profits nothing." It is still only flesh. It is still only the realm of the natural. It is still self.

It is not simply Christ dying for you—it is you dying in Christ! It is not simply Christ being raised from the dead—it is you being raised along with your divine head! It is not simply you reaching out after God—it is God taking the form of man and then, as the Son of Man, changing life's entire process—bringing you out from the tomb charged with the divine life, resurrection life! This is the Christian faith—the faith of the apostles, the "faith of the Son of God."

> *I have been crucified with Christ; it is no longer I who live, but Christ lives in me; and the life which I now live in the flesh I live by faith in the Son of God, who loved me and gave Himself for me.*
>
> *(Gal. 2:20)*

5

Christ's Ascension Our Ascension

I recall a recent visit to the sea after years of seclusion in a barren desert land. When my eyes caught sight of the far horizon, and the great roar of the breakers struck on my heart as the chords of a great organ, I stood speechless.

It is not like that, though, when, after years of weary wandering in the desert land of a self-originated imitation of Christ, you look out for the first time upon the ocean of unfathomable riches which being in Christ holds for you. You are not simply speechless. Like Saul of Tarsus, you fall to earth blinded by the heavenly vision.

I must confess that when I first contemplated what we are about to consider, I staggered. Could it be that even this— Christ's ascension—was mine? Not hereafter, but now? Dared I mount this fiery chariot and like Elijah be swept into glory? Did the Scriptures actually teach such a thing? And how could one be upon earth and yet with Christ in the heavenlies? A thousand questions surged up, demanding a reply. But the

Holy Spirit, who leads us into these mysteries, gave faith. I believed, and now I know. "Faith is more than sight," as Hudson Taylor was accustomed to saying. "It is the *substance* of things hoped for." We come actually to possess the very substance, the pith and the marrow of these unseen realities.

We are made not only partakers of Christ's death and resurrection, but even of His very ascension. As Paul puts it, we were "made to sit together in the heavenlies with Christ Jesus" (Eph 2:6). Jesus states the case in His prayer, in these words:

I in them, and You in Me. . .Father, I desire that they also whom You gave Me may be where I am, that they may behold My glory.

That He had in mind His going to the Father is evident enough, for He had already said: "Now I am no longer in the world. . .But now I come to You." By faith He was already taking His place at the right hand of the Father. He was returning—by the way of the Cross, the empty tomb and *ascension*—returning to the throne He had left. And by faith He was taking with Him those who in the foreknowledge of God were to form His mystical body. The heavenly Bridegroom was placing the bride at His side on the throne.

Believers and Christ are one. Therefore, the Savior could say, "And You have loved them as You have loved Me." For this purpose Christ had come: to graft into Himself a new stock; as Son of Man to constitute Himself head of a new race; as Second Adam to be federal head of a new humanity. And as this new man (the body) would participate in His cross and in the resurrection, so he would also ascend with Him into heaven.

> *God judges us dead, raised, and seated with Christ in the heavenlies. He has blessed us with every spiritual blessing in the heavenly places in Christ.* *(Eph. 1:3)*

We do well to look at the tenses of the verbs which the Holy Spirit employs, as F. B. Meyer points out. *It is ours now:* He *has blessed us* with every spiritual blessing in the heavenly places in Christ. It is not death (physical dissolution) which will bring us into our heritage in Christ. It is faith. We may *now* sit with Him in the heavenlies, because God has *already* made us to sit there in the person of Christ, the head of the church.

If this seems too much, too great a blessing for such unworthy children, let us not forget that the merest crumb of spiritual blessing comes in the same way. It is only because we are *in Christ* that we presume to address the Father at all. Since it would be just as impossible to attain the *least* without Christ, why shall we not attain the *highest* with Him? "He who did not spare His own Son, but delivered Him up for us all, how shall He not with Him also freely give us all things?" Yes, even the throne.

To him who overcomes I will grant to sit with
Me on My throne, as I also overcame and sat
down with My Father on His throne.

(Rev. 3:21)

Yes, this can be our experience here and now!

Dr. G. A. Peck, for some years a missionary in Africa, wrote a book on what he called *Throne Life*, or *Life in the Heavenlies*, in which he expounded this phase of the Christian life in a unique way. He stated that the believer *before* entering into glory through the portals of death may take his place with Christ in the heavenlies and draw upon the Savior's throne life.

Doctor Peck saw the conquest of Canaan, the entrance of the children of Israel into the land of milk and honey, as the great Old Testament type. Canaan represents the highest union with Christ, the throne life to which every believer is called. Joshua represents the Holy Spirit who quickens and imparts faith and leads the believer into this union with Christ. The Canaanites, sons of Anak, giants, etc., represent the mighty forces of evil, satanic and otherwise, which oppose the believer in his attempt to "take" the land of promise—i.e., to take his place with Christ in the heavenlies. As to Joshua, the Lord said, "Every place that the sole of your foot shall tread upon *I have given you.*" So to the believer, the Spirit says, "Blessed be the God and Father of our Lord Jesus Christ, who *has blessed* us with every spiritual blessing in the heavenly places in Christ" (Eph. 1:3).

You are spirit, soul, and body. "The God of peace Himself," prays Paul, "sanctify you completely; and may your whole spirit, soul and body be preserved blameless" (1 Thess. 5:23). The Bible constantly distinguishes between spirit and soul. We are told that the Word of God pierces to the division of soul and spirit (Heb. 4:12). When man fell he ceased to live in the spirit, which is the seat of God-consciousness and which God intended should dominate. He sank into "the vessel of the soul," and then into the flesh. He became "flesh." We read that the Lord was sorry that He had made man; and He said: ". . .for he is indeed flesh" (Gen. 6:3).

Now the purpose of God in the great work of redemption brings you more to a God-consciousness through the spirit; quickens and releases your spirit, disentangling it from that which is soulish and fleshly, and brings it once more into ascendancy so that you might be dominated by the spirit.

So the Cross must cut—dividing asunder soul and spirit. The spirit, once released from the bondage of the fallen life, takes its place with Christ in the heavenlies. Your life should then flow in a steady stream from the throne. Your spirit is translated into the kingdom of Christ *here and now*. During His earthly ministry Jesus stood in just such relations; He could say, "No one has ascended to heaven but he who came down from heaven, that is, the Son of Man *who is in heaven*." As to His spirit, Jesus was in heaven even while He walked on earth and preached by the shores of Galilee. His life flowed in an unceasing stream from the throne.

Now when by faith you rise to claim your place in the

heavenlies, your spirit is released from the bondage of the fallen life. You are disentangled also from the "soulish-life." You are no longer in servitude to self. You are set free. Your life is no longer lived at the circumference. It flows from the center to the circumference.

Christians are living on starvation rations, when all the time the King would have them so filled, so charged with the life of God, so rooted in divine fullness that, unable to contain themselves, rivers of living water would be bursting forth and flowing out to a perishing world! So speaks the Beloved (Christ) in Solomon's Song to the spouse (the bride, the church, or the Christian):

> *A garden enclosed is my sister. . . a spring . . .*
> *a fountain. . . . Your plants are an orchard of*
> *pomegranates with pleasant fruits, fragrant*
> *henna with spikenard, . . . myrrh and aloes*
> *with all chief spices—a fountain of gardens, a*
> *well of living waters, and streams from*
> *Lebanon.*
>
> *(Song of Solomon 4:12-15)*

6

Christ's Victory Our Victory

At no time in your pilgrimage are you free from peril. Temptations of all sorts beset your path. The farther along the road, and the greater the grace, the more subtle the snares and the more intense the opposition.

It is when you realize your position of death-identification with the Lord, rising with Him in spirit to a place of real power, that you come to appreciate the meaning of Paul's words:

> *For we do not wrestle with flesh and blood,*
> *but against principalities, against powers,*
> *against the rulers of the darkness of this age,*
> *against spiritual hosts of wickedness in the*
> *heavenly places.*
>
> *(Eph. 6:12)*

It is then that you begin to grasp the deeper significance of the Cross of Jesus Christ.

Jesus came not merely to reveal the Father's love—to express in terms of human life the divine purpose. He came not only to heal and to teach. Nor was His aim simply to give His life upon the Cross as a ransom for many. In the strictest sense, those were secondary objects. There was one supreme purpose of which little was said, because man in his blindness would not understand. Behind the scenes there was being enacted a mighty drama. Jesus saw Satan fall as lightning from heaven. He saw the real enemy. Not for a second was He deceived. Men were under the dominion of the powers of darkness. The Lord's supreme glory and prime value as our Redeemer, lay in the fact that He was able to break that power. He cast out demons. He faced the enemy in the desert and came forth victor.

It is significant that on the last night before Calvary the Savior should have interpreted His Cross in terms of conflict with the satanic dominion. He said:

> *Now is the judgment of this world; now the ruler of this world will be cast out.*
>
> *(John 12:31)*

Paul had insight into this fact for he wrote that Jesus, through death, had destroyed him who had the power of death, that is, the devil (Heb. 2:14). Elsewhere in speaking of the Savior's Cross he declares that it was there on Calvary that He disarmed principalities and powers and made a public spectacle of them, triumphing over them (Col 2:14-16).

Even so, Satan still has right of access to God above, where he delights in accusing people. And how are we to gain the victory? Through Calvary—by means of "the blood of the Lamb and by the word of [our] testimony" (Rev. 12:11). For *His* victory there is *ours*!

But it not God omnipotent? Why could He not with one stroke have upset the whole satanic hierarchy? He could have, but that would not have answered His purpose nor solved the problem. Man had sinned. Man had been deceived by the great father of lies. So it was necessary that man *of his own free will* should *break* with Satan and *return* to the Father. Therefore, Christ *as man* must overcome *Satan*. Herein lies the virtue of it all: It was essential that the Son of Man, employing weapons which *man* might use, be triumphant.

This conflict cost the Savior the ignominy and shame of the Cross. No man was ever hated as was Jesus—just as no one was ever loved as was He. This hatred for Jesus—the one who befriended thousands, communicating treasures of priceless value—remains the greatest enigma of history.

But what has all this to do with our participation in Christ? Much, every way. You are not only baptized into Christ's death and raised with Him in the power of an endless life, you are a *participant* in His victory over the forces of hell. When the Son of Man achieved, you potentially achieved in Him! The humblest believer may trample the "dragon" under foot. The weakest disciple who realizes his oneness with Christ may, in His name, "bind the strong man" and spoil him of his goods.

The humblest believer who realizes his oneness with Christ is invested with the very authority of the Son of God. As members of His body, we share His executive authority. Shall we not judge angels? If God be for us, who can be against us! Yes, truly, mountains *do* move and are cast into the sea at our bidding. The apostles exercised this power and *we too* may exercise it. Christ stands ready to make effective the command of the humblest lamb of His flock, *if that lamb is obedient.* But we cannot have all that Christ has for us in this regard until He has all of us!

A little bit of self may seem insignificant to us, but God sees it in the light of the Cross. Self is still a monster, and until self is dethroned by the Lord Jesus—dethroned with the actual slaying accomplished by the Cross of Christ—we rob ourselves of infinite wealth and power. God grant to us a disposition to die with Christ so that with Him we may *reign*—in which case the very demons will be subject unto us.

As I look back at the years of my ministry, I shudder at times. I ministered the Cross of Christ, but at times I was oppressed by the enemy. A Christian worker, and oppressed by Satan—the irony of it! But the faithful Shepherd saw my plight and came to my rescue. He gave me light and patient training in the use of weapons which "are not carnal, but mighty in God."

Satan fears only one thing—the Cross of Christ. I do not refer to a mere symbol. I refer to all that Calvary signifies: Christ's victory over the powers of darkness. . .His substitutionary death for the sin of the world. . .the believer's oneness with Christ in death. This is the "Rock cleft for me," in which, if I hide, I shall find shelter from the wiles of the wicked one; against which the gates of hell shall never prevail.

For those who feel themselves still victimized, for those who, in a word, are not wholly free, I would offer the following suggestions.

First: You must "remove all ground." Avail yourself of the power of Christ's Cross. The ground is removed by an assertion of your right to full participation in all the fruits of the victory of Calvary. You must deliberately take your stand with Christ on victory ground; must affirm what God says is true as regards your oneness with Christ in death and resurrection; must deliberately refuse all ground to Satan, and in the name of the Victor of Calvary take back the ground that may have been lost. You must claim in Jesus' name the ground which belongs to the rightful King.

You have been made a participant of Christ, and you have an invincible claim, a blood-bought right, a glorious right springing from your oneness with the Victor of Calvary— a perfect right to freedom. Are not these the good tidings which Jesus came to proclaim? Does He not proclaim liberty to the captives, and the opening of the prison to them that are bound? Did He not cry out from the Cross, "It is finished?" Is it only a ten percent, or a fifty percent, or a ninety percent salvation which He accomplished at so great a cost; or is it an all-inclusive, one hundred percent authentic salvation.

See His trip from glory, the infinite humiliation of the Incarnation; see the ignominy of the Cross. This salvation represents the victory of Calvary.

Arise and take your place with Christ in the heavenlies, "far above all principalities and powers." Your right to the air you breathe and the water you drink is no more inalienable. You are a member of Christ's body, and by the promise of God, a sharer in the covenant of Calvary. You are the legal possessor of all that Christ Himself rose out of the grave to inherit. When God raised His Son from the dead and "seated Him at His right hand in the heavenly places, far above all principality and power and might and dominion, and every name that is named, not only in this age but also in that which is to come, and put *all things under His feet*," you too, member of the body of Christ—you who believe in Him and who have been grafted into the Vine; you, of whom Jesus said, "I in them, and You in Me, that they may be made perfect in One"—you too were raised to sit at the right hand of God. All things have been placed under your feet.

"Awake, you who sleep, arise from the dead, and Christ will give you light." You are not to let go of any of your faculties and expect God to control you as if you were machines. Union with Christ does not suggest any such thing. After coming into deepest union with Christ, so that like Paul you say "I have been crucified with Christ. . .Christ lives in me," you do no become passive. You do not give up self-control. As never before, you *live*. Personality is vastly enhanced. The will is greatly fortified. The mind is marvelously illumined. The memory is gloriously strengthened. You are free as never before to choose, to will, to reason, and to act.

You are now able to act in harmony with God, every faculty energized by the Holy Spirit.

7

Christ's Sufferings Our Sufferings

It is striking how over and over the concept of participation in Christ appears in the New Testament. We are told that we are made partakers of Christ. In Romans 6 we are given to understand that His cross is our cross; His tomb, our tomb. In Ephesians 2 we are made to see that in Him we were raised from the dead and actually made to sit with Him in the heavenlies. Not only that, we are assured again and again that Christ's victory is our victory, that we may always overcome the wicked one because of Calvary, and that we now participate in the glorious fruits of the Cross (2 Cor. 2:14-16).

And now again we are startled by the astounding fact that we are chosen to be partakers of Christ's sufferings. Peter bids us to *rejoice* over this fact. He would have us be glad because we have been called to share the tribulations of the glorified Savior. "Rejoice to the extent that you partake of Christ's sufferings" (1 Pet. 4:13).

Paul, the great apostle of the indwelling Christ, was in the habit of interpreting his trials and tribulations as a Christian, and as an apostle, in the light of the Cross. He saw in them a prolongation of Christ's own sufferings. To the Colossians, he wrote:

I now rejoice in my sufferings for you, and fill up in my flesh what is lacking in the afflictions of Christ, for the sake of His body, which is the church.

(Col. 1:24)

He recognized that it was Christ suffering in and through him.

You are not, of course, to think of this suffering as having anything to do with the burden He bore as our Sin-Bearer, when "the Lord laid on Him the iniquity of us all."

This Man, after He had offered one sacrifice for sins forever, sat down at the right hand of God. *(Heb. 10:12)*

We have been sanctified through the offering of the body of Jesus Christ once for all.

(Heb. 10:10)

By one offering He has perfected forever those who are being sanctified.

(Heb 10:14)

At the time of this cosmic achievement, the Savior Himself cried out with a great voice that rent the rocks: "It is finished!" Nothing can be added to the work consummated on the Cross. Christ died for our sins. All the chorus of inspired voices are pitched to this major key.

Do not confuse the sufferings of Christ of which *we* are partakers with the completed work of Calvary. I repeat, nothing can ever be added to that absolute consummation. "Nothing in my hand I bring, simply to Thy cross I cling." In that all-sufficient sacrifice for sin the believer had no part. He can only accept the forgiveness which issues from the Cross.

Neither confuse these sufferings of Christ with the objective fact of our identification with Christ in His death, as set forth in Romans 6. That also is a completed thing. We are commanded to simply reckon on it as a consummated, historic fact, just as we count on the fact of Christ's death for us. Believe what God has to say about your oneness with His Son in His death to sin; then, on the ground of God's Word, simply refuse the old life as if it were an utterly powerless thing. It really is, because of your being with Christ in His death. You are released from the bondage of self. Your old life drops off like a decayed garment. You are now *alive unto* God. *And now in the power of this new divine life,* as a member of Christ's body, there comes to you as an inevitable consequence, a participation in Christ's sufferings.

Because your life now issues from the throne. . .because, in spirit, you are virtually seated in the heavenlies. . .and because, as never before, you are one with Christ—as the result of all this you discover working within you a new spirit of love. And the love of Christ constraining you inevitably issues in a great suffering.

Do not imagine, therefore, that because of your oneness with Christ in the heavenlies you are brought into some fool's paradise which exempts you from further suffering. The truth of the matter is that it simply increases your capacity for suffering many thousandfold. You begin to carry about in your body the dying of the Lord Jesus (2 Cor. 4:10).

Rejoice inasmuch as you are made a partaker of Christ's sufferings. The great fact is that we are *all* to bear the Savior's image; we are to be conformed to His death. In the power of His resurrection we are to have the fellowship of His sufferings, being made conformable unto His death (Phil. 3:10).

And, praise God, this suffering is not without its precious fruit. Christ turns it all to your account. He uses it to prune the branches of the vine that they may bear more fruit (John 15:2). Nothing touches you without first passing through His hands and being made to serve your highest eternal interests. Why do you bear in your body "the dying of the Lord Jesus?" That the life of Jesus also may be manifested in your body (2 Cor. 4:10).

How are these "rivers of living water" to flow from your innermost being except the outer self be broken? The grape does not yield its precious juice without the breaking of the outer wall. The walls of selfhood must be leveled if you are to yield your life in exchange for the life of Jesus. That is why the Holy Spirit turns you over to death:

For we who live are always delivered to death
for Jesus' sake, that the life of Jesus also may
be manifested in our mortal flesh.   So then
death is working in us, but life in you.

(2 Cor. 4:11-12)

What a blessed message for the afflicted soul.   Lift up
your head, for your redemption draws nigh!   It is not in vain
that you suffer.   There can be no gold without the refiners fire.
Christ is glorified in your patience.   You are bidden to count it
all joy when you experience various testings (Jas. 1:2).   From
your wounds healing streams of life—Christ's own life—are
flowing.   This will bring about the increase and edification of
Christ's body.   What you suffer will deepen your "death-
identification position" with Christ.   The kernel of wheat must
fall into the ground and die, else it abides alone.

O you afflicted one, tossed with tempest and
not comforted, behold, I will lay your stones
with colorful gems, and lay your foundations
with sapphires.   I will make your pinnacles of
rubies, your gates of crystal, and all your walls
of precious stones.   All your children shall be
taught by the Lord, and great shall be the peace
of your children.

(Isa. 54:11-13)

For as the sufferings of Christ abound in us, so our consolation also abounds through Christ.

(2 Cor. 1:5)

8

Christ's Appearing Our Appearing

We have not yet exhausted the deep veins of purest gold
to which this principle of participation in Christ has led us. In
a sense, the most sublime of all its aspects has to do with the
future developments of Christ's kingdom. There is the great
fact of the Savior's Second Coming about which the New
Testament has so much to say. We are told to watch and pray,
for we know not what hour our Lord may come (Matt.26:41).
We are told to abide in Him that when He shall appear we may
have confidence and not be ashamed before Him at His coming
(1 John 2:28). We are told that the angels shall be sent forth
with a great sound of the trumpet, and that they shall gather
together the elect from the four winds (Matt. 24:31).

The Second Coming may have been abused and distorted
out of proportion to other truths, but what word of our Lord
has not been abused? As disciples of Christ, we dare not be
indifferent to any truth; nor dare we neglect any word that
ever issued from the lips of our Lord. Again and again, the

Lord declared He would come again. The inspired writers with one voice announce His glorious appearing as the consummate event toward which all history is moving. This cannot be denied.

Now, just because you may not be able to grasp the full significance of the Savior's word, or understand just what this glorious appearing may involve, are you going to turn aside from the comfort which this great hope imparts? Are you going to ignore the promise, "When He is revealed we shall be like Him, and everyone who has this hope purifies himself, even as He is pure," because you cannot comprehend some aspects of His return?

Is the Lord worthy of trust only when He is understood? Will you follow only when the intellect can support you? Is it any more astounding than those things which have already transpired—the Incarnation, the raising of Lazarus, the Cross, the empty tomb, the Ascension, your oneness with Christ in death and resurrection?

What of the prophets—did they understand the full import of the revelation given to them regarding the first coming of Christ? They did not understand. The marvelous events which transpired in Galilee—the proclamation of which, even after two thousand years, still causes the ears of the world to tingle— were no less baffling to them, as from ancient times they looked forward to them, than the unfulfilled prophecies to which you look forward in your day.

I am not ashamed to confess that I do not understand. But I do believe.

I have come to realize my oneness with Christ in death and resurrection and have come to enjoy the full fruits of His victory on Calvary. I now partake in the ascension of my Lord as one who has been made to sit with Him in the heavenlies. My sufferings as a follower of Christ are a filling up of His sufferings.

Now that the everlasting gospel has done its work in me, I look forward as never before to the coming of my King. Could it be otherwise, when I know that even in that supreme event I shall participate? When Christ who is our life returns then we will also appear with Him in glory (Col.3:4).

He can do nothing without us! We are His body.

Christ has bound us to Himself with ties so strong that we are all members of His body. You do not speak of your own hand as being far away or near. . .your hand is a part of your body. You undertake a project with the full participation of every member of your body.

The Lord Jesus Christ has bound you so eternally and utterly to Himself that when He moves, you move.

Of course, you shall appear with Him! It could not be otherwise. You are a part of His body. The church is one with the Lord. We are one with the eternal Godhead.

The glory of this mystic oneness with Christ! To what an indescribable destiny it commits us. No longer concern yourself about whether or not you shall go to heaven. (If Christ is not there, you would rather not go.) Jesus Christ *is* heaven!

The faintest glimmer of light from His holy countenance— beside which the sun is but a shadow—suffices your heart.

While in prison, it was just that glimmer of the Lord, that enabled Paul and Silas to rejoice. Paul's back was bleeding . . .he was in prison. . .it was the dead of night. But Paul sings as one who is in Christ. Heaven's glorious light bursts in about him, and he forgets all but his Lord.

You will participate in Christ's coming.

You will be caught up.

You will be changed!

Chariots of fire will sweep you from the earth in a twinkling of an eye. This one thing is still to come; Christ's eternal plan is not yet complete; Paul declares that there is a great groaning in nature. One writer has referred to it as the trinity of groanings: The whole creation groans. . .the spirit groans. . . you groan. For what? For the redemption of your body (Rom. 8:23).

Your body is to be changed. You are to be glorified with Christ. As His body was glorified, so your body will be glorified *in Him.*

> *As we have borne the image of the man of dust, we shall also bear the image of the heavenly Man. . .Behold, I tell you a mystery: We shall not all sleep, but we shall all be changed—in a moment, in the twinkling of an eye, at the last trumpet. For the trumpet will sound, and the dead will be raised incorruptible, and we shall be changed. For this corruptible must*

put on incorruption, and this mortal must put
on immortality. So when this corruptible has
put on incorruption, and this mortal has put
on immortality, then shall be brought to pass
the saying that is written: "Death is swallowed
up in victory"...Thanks be to God, who gives
us the victory through our Lord Jesus Christ.
(1 Cor. 15:49-57)

We are moving forward toward the most stupendous transactions in the history of the human race. I do not wish to be dogmatic and quarrel over the interpretation of dispensational truth. It behooves all Christians to be exceedingly tolerant as to one another's mode of interpreting the Word in its bearing on the future. Some believe that the shadow of the Great Tribulation is already upon us: that we may be caught up at any moment. Others tell us that the event may not transpire for thousands of years. Be all that as it may. No one knows for sure but the Father.

One thing, however, is clear. We are to be *participants* in Christ's coming. Nothing can befall Him that does not befall us. We are yet to participate in a fuller measure in the glorious fruits of redemption. We shall be *like* Him, for we shall see Him as He is. With Him we shall *reign*. The stream of life which proceeds from the throne and from the Lamb, and which breaks in upon us so that even now "rivers of living water" flow from our innermost being, is going to just overflow all its banks someday, so that the enemy Death will be literally *swallowed up in victory.*

Our ascension with Christ will not be merely in spirit as it is now; our participation in the ascension will blossom forth in its true splendor—and then we shall shine as the sun forever in the kingdom of the Father.

> *And I heard, as it were, the voice of a great multitude, as the sound of many waters and as the sound of mighty thundering, saying, "Alleluia! For the Lord God Omnipotent reigns! Let us be glad and rejoice and give Him glory, for the marriage of the Lamb has come, and His wife has made herself ready"*
> *. . .Then he said to me, "Write: Blessed are those who are called to the marriage supper of the Lamb!" And he said to me, "These are the true sayings of God."*
>
> *(Rev. 19.6-9)*

You will have your part in the yet unfilled history of Christ. For as you have been made to partake of the death of the founder of the New Race, and in Him were resurrected and made to sit in the heavenlies in spirit, so, in that sublime event toward which the church moves—the marriage supper of the Lamb—you too shall participate.

Thanks be to God for His unspeakable gift!

9

Discovery and Experience

Live your Christian life on the basis of *participation* in Christ, not *imitation* of Christ.

I have for many years been a lover of biography. In my studies, I recently came upon what I shall call a typical case . . .in the experience of the founder of the China Inland Mission.

Whether one agrees or not with the missionary principles laid down by Hudson Taylor, an unbiased study of his life and work reveals that he was one of the great Christian workers of recent history. His achievements were colossal. At a time when the interior of China was closed to foreigners, and when ignorance, fanaticism, and race prejudice made it exceedingly hazardous to venture into the interior of China, Dr. Taylor established a chain of missions in almost all the great provinces of the interior. The church records no more amazing story of sacrifice and of achievement than that of the humble doctor who laid the foundations of the kingdom of God in the interior of China!

But Hudson Taylor was not always victorious, not always that joyous expounder of the faith which in the later period of his life all who came to know him found him to be. The fact of the matter is that even though he had already achieved great things as a missionary, and had mightily influenced the church in the homeland—and was highly esteemed as a man of God by Christian leaders of many lands—yet, in his letters to loved ones he often pours out the pain of his soul over the fact of his spiritual poverty.

There is a hidden plague in his heart. He is consumed by secret longings. Like Paul, he cries out "O wretched man that I am! Who will deliver me from this body of death?" He longs to be victorious over sin. He struggles, he agonizes. In spite of all his efforts, sin as a principle continues to master him; the Savior is no more real to him than before. He cannot, in the true sense, overcome. If ever a man strove to imitate the Master, he was than man! But all to no avail.

In 1869, a great change took place. It was so radical, so complete, so overwhelming, that all of Mr. Taylor's fellow-workers were soon aware of the fact. A tide of divine life swept through the mission as a result. So great a change had been wrought that, in all the doctor's attitudes—his correspondence, his sermons, his prayer life, his very purposes—a new light shone forth.

I quote from a letter by Mr. Judd: "He was a joyous man now, a bright, happy Christian. He had been a toiling, burdened one before, with not much rest of soul. He was resting now in Jesus, and letting Him do the work—which makes all the difference. Whenever he spoke in meetings after that, life seemed to flow from him; and in practical things a new peace possessed him. Troubles did not worry him as before. He cast everything on God in a new way and gave more time to prayer. . .from him flowed the living water to others.

"When I went to welcome him," wrote Mr. Judd, "he was so full of joy that he scarcely knew how to speak to me. He did not even say 'How do you do?' but walking up and down the room with his hands behind him, exclaimed, 'Oh, Mr. Judd, God has made me a new man! God has made me a new man.'"

To his sister he wrote: "I feel as though the first glimmer of the dawn of a glorious day has arisen upon me. I hail it with trembling, yet with trust."

But what caused this great change? I draw somewhat at length from a letter written to his sister on October 17, 1869:

". . .as to work, mine was never so plentiful, so responsible, or so difficult; but the weight and strain are all *gone*. The last month has been perhaps the happiest of my life; and I long to tell you a little of what the Lord has done for my soul. . .

"I hated myself. I hated my sin; and yet, I gained no strength against it. I felt I *was* a child of God: His Spirit in my heart would cry, 'Abba Father'; but to rise to my privileges as a child, I was utterly powerless.

"All the time I felt assured there was in Christ all I needed, but the practical question was how was I to get it *out*? I knew full well that there was in the Root abundant fatness; but how to get in into my puny little branch was the question. As the light gradually dawned on me, I saw that faith was the only prerequisite—was the hand to lay hold on His fullness and make it my own. *But I had not this faith!* I strove for it but it would not come; tried to exercise it, but in vain. Seeing more and more the wondrous supply laid up in Jesus, the fullness of our precious Savior, my helplessness and guilt seemed to increase. Sins committed seemed but as trifles compared with the sin of unbelief which was their cause—which could not, or would not, take God at His word, but rather made Him a liar. Unbelief was, I felt, the damning sin of the world—yet, I indulged in it. . .

"When my agony of soul was at its height, a sentence in a letter from dear McCarthy was used to remove the scales from my eyes, and the Spirit of God revealed the truth of our *oneness* with Jesus as I had never known it before. McCarthy, who had been exercised by the same sense of failure, but saw the light before I did, wrote: 'But how to get faith strengthened? Not by striving after faith, but by resting on the Faithful One.' As I read I saw it all: 'If we believe not, He abideth faithful.' I looked to Jesus and saw (and when I saw, oh, how joy flowed!) that He had said: 'I will never leave you.' Ah! there is rest, I thought. I have striven in vain to rest in Him. I'll strive no more. For has He not promised to abide with me?

"But this was not all He showed me, nor one-half. As I thought of the Vine and the branches, what light the blessed Spirit poured direct into my soul: I saw not only that Jesus would never leave me, but that I was a member of His body, of His flesh, and of His bones. The Vine, now I see, is not the root merely, but all—root, stem, branches, twigs, leaves, flowers, fruit. And Jesus is not only that: He is soil and sunshine, air and showers, and ten thousand times more than we have every dreamed, wished for, or needed. Oh! the joy of seeing this truth. I do pray that the eyes of your understanding may be enlightened, that you may know and enjoy the riches freely given us in Christ."

And now comes the part bearing yet more directly upon the subject in hand:

"Oh! my dear sister, it is a wonderful thing to be really one with a risen and exalted Savior; to be a member of Christ. Think what it involves. Can Christ be rich and I poor? Can your right hand be rich and the left poor? Or your head be well-fed while your body starves? Again, think of its bearing on prayer. Could a bank clerk say to a customer, 'It was only your hand which wrote that check, not you,' or, 'I cannot pay this sum to your hand, but only to yourself'? No more can your prayers or mine be discredited if offered in the name of Jesus (i.e., not in your own name, or for the sake of Jesus merely, but on the ground that we are His members) so long as we keep within the extent of Christ's credit—a very wide limit.

"The sweetest part, if one may speak of one part being sweeter than another, is the *rest* which full identification with Christ brings. I am no longer anxious about anything. . .for He, I know, is able to carry out His will, and His will is mine. It makes no matter where He places me or how. That is rather for Him to consider than for me. For the easiest positions, He must give me grace; and in the most difficult, His grace is also sufficient. It makes little difference to my servant whether I send him to buy a few cents worth of things or the most expensive articles. In either case, he looks to me for the money and brings me the purchases. So, if God places me in great perplexity, must He not give me much guidance? In positions of great difficulty, much grace? In circumstances of great pressure and trial, much strength? His resources are mine, for He is mine. . .*all this springs from the believer's oneness with Christ.*

"I am no better than before (I do not wish to be, nor am I striving to be); *but I am dead and buried with Christ, and risen too, and ascended;* and now Christ lives in me, 'and the life I now live in the flesh, I live by the faith of the Son of God, who loved me and gave Himself for me.' I now believe *I am dead to sin.* God reckons me so, and tells me to reckon myself so—and He knows best. All my past experience may have shown that it was not so; but dare I now say it is not true, when He says it *is?* I feel and know that old things have passed away. I am as capable of sinning as ever, but now I realize Christ is present, as never before. He cannot sin and He can keep me from sinning.

"I cannot say that since I have seen this light I have not sinned, but I do feel that there was no need to have done so. And further—walking more in the light, my conscience has been more tender; sin has been instantly confessed and pardoned; and peace and joy instantly restored. . ."

I have quoted at considerable length from Mr. Taylor's

correspondence, because his experience illustrates so strikingly the incalculable difference which this principle of identification with Christ makes. He had been a burdened Christian; he becomes a joyous, triumphant one. He had been a Christian who strove and agonized in the energy of the old life to be Christ like, only to be brought at last to utter self-despair. He realizes, at last, his position of identification with Christ in death and resurrection, and there emerges a new man, who is swept forward by the tide of a divine life, and who no longer serves mechanically, from a mere sense of duty, but spontaneously from the inner surgings of a heavenly life.

Had Mr. Taylor written for the very purpose of giving us something that would illustrate in perfect detail the force of what we have attempted to set forth, he could not have offered us anything more to the point.

The discovery of his union with Christ in death and resurrection *revolutionized* the life and work of a great pioneer in Christian work. And, wherever it is seen and faithfully acted upon, wherever this oneness with the Savior is realized in actual experience, whether it be by the humblest believer or the greatest Christian leader, the same glorious results must follow! Defeat will give place to victory. Spiritual poverty will turn to riches of grace and fullness of life. Weakness will give place to power. A mechanical striving to imitate Christ will be changed into a delightful spontaneity in the participation of His divine life.

Should you come to know your Lord in this way, your

gnawing sense of insufficiency will be transformed into a glorious all-sufficiency—in a deep union with the all-sufficient Christ!

This is the happy fulfillment of the wonderful promise found in the ninth chapter of 2 Corinthians:

> *And God is able to make all grace abound toward you, that you, always having all sufficiency in all things, may have an abundance for every good work.*
>
> *(2 Cor. 9:8)*

10

The Church and Oneness in Christ

The relationship of oneness with Christ which we have been considering is revolutionary. It calls for radical changes in all phases of your Christian life. As never before, "old things have passed away and all things have become new." You have become "a new creation." The old life has been terminated by the Cross of Christ. And an ever-deeper participation in the Cross results in an ever-fuller experience of the power of the resurrection.

That this new life in Christ will greatly affect your relation to the church as a visible reality is, of course, to be expected. In one sense it unhinges you. Your attachment to the true church, which is the mystical body of Christ, becomes so deep and so real that you feel yourself somewhat detached from the visible church as it has been organized (perhaps I should say disorganized) by man.

In dying to your fallen life, you naturally die to all that is *nurtured* by the old life. This means that the church itself, regarded as a visible organization, simply fails to grip you to whatever extent it is out of line with the Holy Spirit and is giving place to the life of the flesh, as revealed in strife, hurt feelings, arguing, defending yourself, sectarian pride, class distinctions, unsound doctrines, racial superiority and the like. In this state, the organization does not attract you, as it fails to express the mind of Christ.

You die to every aspect of walking in the flesh, whether in gatherings of the church or in your simple routines of daily living.

The tie which now binds you to *Christ* is so strong that you find yourself bound to all those who, regardless of denominational affiliations, are enjoying a like precious faith. You experience a spiritual oneness as deep and as precious with other Christians who have been rooted into Christ as you do with those of your own church. It is no longer a question of ecclesiastical procedure, but of life.

The rising tide of divine life is forever overflowing all of its banks in you who have learned to stand in Christ. Once it rises high enough it simply wipes out ecclesiastical barriers; the mighty walls between believers, no matter their denominations, disappear. You could no more realize a deep oneness with Christ in death and resurrection and not realize a profound oneness with all those who receive the same influx of heavenly life than you could be a member of some particular family and not be bound to the members of that family.

You are seated with Christ in heavenly places, and from this rampart you look out upon life, conscious that you are free from its petty strife. Race prejudices can no longer touch you. Class distinctions have been swept away. Sectarian grooves can no longer contain your sympathies. Christ's cross has created for us a new and harmonious universe.

Our love (the love of Christ in us) flows out in yearning love toward others. The Beloved, the Bridegroom, says "Come away with me, my spouse."

Would a bride be content with the outer trappings—a ring, a church ceremony, legal recognition, etc., if her husband is living in whoredom? Does she not rightfully expect fellowship, faithfulness, love, purity—in a word, oneness of spirit with her beloved? Will our heavenly Bridegroom be satisfied with ceremonies, forms and symbols if we are not His *in spirit?*

Our Savior took you with Himself to the Cross to annihilate forever your fallen life and all that might come between Him and you, so that He might unite you to Himself in holy, spiritual wedlock. Dare you offer Him the trappings and withhold the reality?

> *Let no one judge you in food or in drink, or regarding a festival or a new moon or Sabbaths, which are a* shadow *of things to come, but the* substance *is of* Christ.
>
> *(Col. 2:16-17)*

11

The Christian Worker and Oneness with Christ

It is in the life and work of the Christian worker that the effect of this position in Christ is most telling. It is here that I have myself put to the test this principle of identification with Christ in death and resurrection. The result has been so overwhelmingly satisfying, so far-reaching, so incalculably blessed, that I look upon the years prior to experiencing the power of the Cross as well-nigh wasted. I walked with an uncertain step; I aimed at an uncertain goal; I employed uncertain weapons; I garnered exceedingly unsatisfying fruits. I see now that much of my labor was not only unsatisfactory but positively harmful.

I preached Christ in the power of a self-originated fervor and consequently mutilated Him (gave Him no chance to reveal His true self). Christ must be preached in the power of a Christ-centered, Christ-possessed, Christ-empowered life. Christ is never truly preached until the one who bears the message is himself so hidden away with Him in God that it is no longer the messenger who speaks but Christ speaking through him. You must learn to bury yourself in the Savior's wounds, so to speak, and die to your own life if you would present Christ to perishing souls. Rivers of living water must accompany the message, for the listener must be flooded by the divine life if he is to be given a chance to appreciate the Christ of God and see Him in His true glory. Unless the gospel is preached with "the power of the Holy Spirit sent from heaven" it is not the gospel at all, no matter how true the speaker might be to "the letter." "The letter kills, but the Spirit gives life."

Christian leaders in all lands are painfully aware that workers in foreign lands are not duplicating the sort of thing we find in the book of Acts. The great expanding machinery of foreign work moves as never before since the Savior issued the great commission, and yet too often missions are not breaking the power of the old life of heathenism.

The crux of the whole matter lies in the fact that we have not exalted Christ and the Cross. Only a gospel which, as a result of union with Christ, brings worker and other believers to the experience of an inner crucifixion and a glorious resurrection can ever do that. Unless worker as well as other believers experience an inner union with Christ, they may struggle to imitate Him and they may even succeed in glossing over the old man with the veneer of Christian culture; but such a counterfeiting of the Christian life, sincere as it may be, will sooner or later break down under the strain to which it is subjected.

12

The Effect of Oneness with Christ on Prayer

When you come to consider prayer in the light of your oneness with Christ, you find that prayer becomes a whole new experience. Prayer is nothing if it is not fellowship; and true fellowship is only possible when the old life, which cannot have fellowship with God, is terminated.

The reason why many are finding prayer so unsatisfactory and the life of prayer so unattractive is because they have attempted to enter into the celestial realms of prayer in the strength of the old man! The old man can no more wield weapons which "are not carnal but mighty in God" (2 Cor. 10:4) than he can "love his enemies," "rejoice always," or "have the mind which was in Christ Jesus"—or fulfill any other Christian grace. Human nature may imitate these graces, but actually possess them? Never. They are "the fruits of the Spirit." They come from above. They are the outworkings of the Christ-nature imparted to the believer and incorporated into his being on the basis of the Cross.

True prayer can only be experienced on the basis of your participation with Christ in His death, resurrection and ascension. Prayer is a matter of fellowship and abiding (you in Him and He in you). You enter into the fellowship of the triune God as you experience the reality of being *in Christ*. "If you abide in Me and I in you, you will ask what you desire, and it shall be done for you." We must be *in Christ*. But we cannot be in Christ in the fullest sense unless in the power of the Savior's death we commit to death the old life.

It is when you realize your oneness with Christ in death and resurrection that prayer becomes the marvelous force that we find it was in the life of the Savior, the invincible dynamic that it reveals itself to be in the book of Acts, and the ineffable experience of the great saints of the ages. It is then that your spirit as well will "mount up on wings as eagles." It is then that fellowship with God comes spontaneously and naturally to its fullest expression.

Only then does the injunction "Pray without ceasing" cease to be an impossible command. For the spirit, released from captivity to the fallen life and freed from all oppression by entering into the full benefits of the Calvary victory, rises to take its place with its Lover in the heavenlies.

When prayer is energized by the Spirit of the living God, it becomes at times a groaning which is unutterable and which does not fail to move mountains and achieve the impossible. Prayer then becomes a working out of the will of God, and therefore must prevail—be the difficulties what they may, however staggering the problem, however great the need. It is then that the great disparity between what Jesus said prayer would accomplish and the miserable caricature that it is in the actual practice of millions, is removed, and prayer blossoms out in all the glory of its true nature!

Shall we not give place then to a pure Christianity? Christ cannot possess you and cause the promised rivers of living water to flow forth from your heart with healing, transforming force, unless you are willing to be dispossessed of your own life. Christ cannot build His church upon the old foundations of selfishness. It is not a case of simply denying yourselves certain things, but it requires a complete renunciation of yourself.

Christ took you *with Himself* to the Cross. Your Adamic life (fallen life) was potentially terminated at Calvary. Will you not, drawn by that love which so moved the Savior that He was willing to be spat upon, willing to be hung between two criminals while the mob jeered, and willing to die!. . .will you not respond with glad surrender to the yearnings of the Crucified?

He would have you share His cross; He would have you be divorced from fleshly thinking, which is enmity with God, by a participation in His own death. Into His death you have been baptized (Rom. 6:3). If you belong to Christ, then His death to sin is your death to sin—His resurrection, your resurrection—His victory, your victory—His ascension, your ascension! God grant you the grace to claim your full heritage that thus you may be more than conqueror!

Now to Him who is able to keep you from stumbling, and to present you faultless before the presence of His glory with exceeding joy, to God our Savior, who alone is wise, be glory and majesty, dominion and power, both now and forever. Amen.

(Jude 24-25)

ABOUT THE AUTHOR

F. J. Huegel spent more than twenty-five years as a missionary in Mexico. It was during this period in his life that he became well-known for his books on the deeper life. Many of his books became popular in both the United States and Great Britain.

He served as a chaplain during World War I. After the war he gave a great deal of his time to prison evangelism. After he retired from that ministry, he taught at Union Seminary in Mexico City.

Other Books by Gene Edwards

Radical Books for Radical Readers
   Overlooked Christianity
   Beyond Radical
   Rethinking Elders
   Revolution
   The Silas Diary *(coming in Summer of 1998)*
   How To Meet Under The Headship Of Jesus Christ
   When The Church Was Led By Laymen
   Climb The Highest Mountain

Books on the Deeper Christian Life
   The Highest Life
   The Secret To The Christian Life
   The Inward Journey

Books which Inspire
   The Divine Romance
   The Chronicles of the Door:
      The Beginning
      The Escape
      The Birth
      The Triumph
      The Return

Books that Heal
   Crucified by Christians
   The Prisoner in the Third Cell
   A Tale of Three Kings

Available from:
The SeedSowers
P.O.Box 285, Sargent, GA 30275
Ph: 1-800-645-2342

Order From SeedSowers Publishing House

Great Books By Other Authors

Please call and order a book and tape catalogue.

Available from:
The SeedSowers
P.O.Box 285, Sargent, GA 30275
Ph: 800-645-2342